"Too few people have heard of Sor Juana Inés de la Cruz—a poet-philosopher-nun whose creative and intellectual aptitudes thwarted the conventions of her time. Lover of truth and oracle of love, spirited defender of her sex, Sor Juana is a delight to read. Her poems reveal a mind and heart thrumming with life. Rhina Espaillat's lively and lyrical translation is a vital leap forward in bringing Sor Juana out of the shadows of history."

—ABIGAIL FAVALE, author of *The Genesis of Gender*

"Rhina Espaillat is the only translator I know who can render an original poem into English with perfect fidelity. Translation can be a kind of treachery: *traduttore, traditore*. It usually involves a trade-off—between a poem's meaning and the form that is integral to its effect. *The Liquid Pour in which my Heart has Run* reproduces both. The poems do justice to every nuance without injecting anything that isn't there.

Readers are always at the mercy of the translator. But with a poem? Each *word* is freighted with such heavy responsibility! Robert Frost defined poetry as "what gets lost in translation"; Rhina Espaillat finds it every time."

—DEBORAH WARREN, author of *Strange to Say: Etymology for Serious Entertainment* and *Connoisseurs of Worms*

The Liquid Pour in which my Heart has Run

Poems by Sor Juana Inés de la Cruz

Wiseblood Books
P.O. Box 870
Menomonee Falls, WI 53052

Printed in the United States of America

Set in Baskerville URW Typesetting

Cover Design: Amanda Brown

The cover painting is in the collection of Museo de Juana Inès de la Cruz, in Amecameca, Mexico

ISBN 13: 978-1-951319-21-2

The Liquid Pour in which my Heart has Run

Poems by Sor Juana Inés de la Cruz

Mi corazón deshecho entre tus manos

versos de Sor Juana Inés de la Cruz

TRANSLATED BY RHINA P. ESPAILLAT

INTRODUCTION BY SALLY READ

Wiseblood Books

CONTENTS

Introduction by Sally Read
1

A Word from the Translator
9

¿En perseguirme, mundo, qué interesas?
14

When You Pursue Me, World
15

A la esperanza
16

To Hope
17

Con el dolor de la mortal herida
18

In Pain as from a Mortal Wound
19

Al que ingrato
20

Ingrates Who Flee Me
21

El ausente, el celoso, se provoca
22

The Absent and the Jealous Suffer Much
23

Fabio, en el ser de todos adoradas
24

Fabio, in Truth, it is the Wish of All
25

Que no me quiera Fabio
26

Fabio, Who Knows I Love Him
27

Feliciano me adora, y le aborrezco
28

Feliciano, Who Adores Me, I Despise
29

Redondillas
30

Stanzas: The Charge
31

Detente, sombra de mi bien esquivo
40

Hall, Dearest Shadow, Always Poised to Flee
41

Tan grande, ¡ay hado!
42

So Great, O Fortune!
43

Esta tarde, mi bien
44

Today, My Treasure
45

Amor empieza por desasosiego
46

Love Has its Early Stirrings in Unease
47

Dices que yo te olvido, Celio, y mientes
48

You Say that I Forget You, But You Lie
49

Dices, que no te acuerdas, Clori, y mientes
50

You Claim to Have Forgotten Me, But Lie
51

Miró Celia una rosa que en el prado
52

Celia Had Found a Proud Rose in the Field
53

Si los riesgos del mar considerara
54

If One Explored the Risks at Sea
55

Primero sueño (versos 1-18)
56

First Dream (Lines 1-18)
57

Primero sueño (versos 781-826)
58

First Dream (Lines 781-826)
59

Soneto 185: A la muerte del Señor Rey Felipe IV
64

Sonnet 185: On the Death of His Majesty
65

Rosa divina
66

Rose Like a Goddess
67

Este que ves, engaño colorido
68

This That You See, This Brightly-Hued Pretense
69

Acknowledgments
71

About Sor Juana Inés de la Cruz
73

About the Translator
75

About Sally Read
77

INTRODUCTION

What might we expect from the poetry of a seventeenth century nun? Whatever it is, the poems of Sor Juana Inés de la Cruz probably confound those expectations. Their author, who would become known as the "Phoenix of the Americas," is a woman, and a poet, of enigma. Some critics have seen Juana's love poetry as Sapphic. Dodging marriage and creating space for study are cited as reasons for her religious vocation. The poems within these pages cannot explain everything about their author's life, but the aforementioned theories miss the most important aspect of both writer and work: Juana's *uncontrollable* passion for letters—a passion that she thought religious life would snuff out, but which she ultimately defended as a way of bringing her closer to God.

Hunger for learning was innate in Juana. When she was little, this illegitimate Spanish-Creole girl would cut a chunk off the length of her hair for every mistake she made in her Latin studies. She was not in a classroom. There was no exacting teacher beside her. In her grandfather's library she gobbled up books and set herself the task of learning everything that there was to know. No one was harder on her than herself. *Snip!* went the scissors if she messed up.

The odds against this girl becoming one of the great lights of the Spanish Golden Age were still high. But reading Juana's work and about her life, one has the sense of a woman who pours out poetry as a tight faucet shoots out high-pressure water. The time in which Juana was born, and the culture of New Spain, were the constricting faucet; her writing was the irrepressible flood. Juana had to resist being silenced, being censored, being kept in what she described as "holy ignorance." She begged to pursue her education, even suggesting that she dress as a man to go to university. By the time she reached the royal court as a self-educated young woman she was, like Catherine of Alexandria, ready to be grilled by a panel of scholars—and acquitted herself brilliantly. Perhaps, for Juana, limits and prohibition were the whetstone of talent.

And then, in 1667, Juana became a nun. But, once she had found a suitable Order, her holy cell did not mean an end to her creative pursuits. In the convent, Juana amassed one of the largest libraries in the Americas and an enviable collection of scientific and musical instruments. She read, she wrote, she debated, and discussed. The traffic of literature and rhetoric between convent and court was abuzz. We might even say that Juana found her niche in religious life—writing sublime songs dedicated to the Virgin Mary and Catherine of Alexandria, and more of her uniquely intelligent and beautiful poems. When the bishop of Puebla published (without Juana's permission) a critique by Juana of a respected preacher's sermon, and scolded her for it, the poetess penned a response that is one of the first truly feminist tracts, a forerunner of the work of Anglophone feminist writers such as Mary Wollstonecraft and Virginia Woolf. In her essay, Juana seems to instinctively uphold the innate right of women to fulfill their God-given potential—it is a prototypical feminism and one that she was at pains to find confirmed in the tradition of the Catholic Church. She declares herself a daughter of Saint Jerome and Saint Paula. In tones of somewhat histrionic humility and apology (remember that the Inquisition was well underway) she details the spirit of learning within her that could not be stopped, cut, trammeled. A spirit that bloomed like a pruned plant in response to her own punitive scissors. Her urge to learn, she insists, is involuntary. When an abbess prohibited her from studying, the entire universe became her primer, she explains. She wrote poetry and debated even (or especially) while she dreamed. The Mother of God was a poet, she argues. And so was Saint Gregory of Nazianzus. The Catholic Church uses poetry all of the time! Learning and poetry are inescapable for Juana. She is perfectly capable of philosophizing, she insists, while cooking supper. And if Aristotle had cooked stews, and observed "nature's secrets" as she had done, he would have written even more.

Yet, after her scintillating "Response" to the bishop's reprimand, Juana fell silent, only writing in blood her repentance, which began "I the worst of all . . ." She died not long afterwards, having written nothing more.

She leaves us poems (a selection of which are translated here), plays, and songs which sparkle with the ethnic identities, poetic formalities, and rules of love that marked her life. She not only knew Latin. She wrote in Nahuatl. She produced villancicos (traditional songs) and silvas (a traditional form of seven and eleven syllable lines). She wrote sonnets in the Petrarchan form. Her body of work ranks among the greats of the Baroque Golden Age, yet at the same time it encompasses the marginalized. It is female. It uses Nahuatl and Spanish; its subjects are secular and religious. As readers of the English language, her sonnets put us in mind of the "Amoretti" of Edmund Spenser. Her use of rhetoric and image is stellar.

It is with the sonnets that we are mostly concerned in this selection of Juana's work, and their translator, Rhina P. Espaillat, is excellently placed to give us a true rendition of the poems. Bilingual herself, Espaillat has long been mistress of the sonnet form, with which, from its tight formality, she releases a wealth of pathos and insight in her own poetry. We are fortunate to have her as guardian of Juana's work, and interpreter (because translators are always, more or less, interpreters) of her words. Espaillat's great care and bravura with language (which makes even the most complex form seem simple) means she necessarily respects the same in Juana's work, and she easily conveys Juana's meaning in her English words. Espaillat knows that poetic music was very important to Juana, and she never fails to honor this in these translations. She misses nothing of the nun's lyricism, or meaning.

Juana's sonnets abound with names and lovers' games. As all of Juana's poems, aside from "First Dream," were commissioned, we cannot draw conclusions about the real -life state of the courtier's/nun's heart. Love-making and friendship had a different poetic lexicon in those days. But it is clear from these sonnets that Juana loved the rhetoric of love and flirtation; the quasi-scientific reasons for, as Spenser had it, "My love (as being) like to ice and I to fire." In "Ingrates Who Flee Me," Espaillat's translation milks the dexterity of Juana's parallel logic. Alliterative assonance and rhythm power this sonnet through to its neat and hard-won conclusion. Pursuit of a different kind is explored in "When You Pursue Me, World" in which we hear what seems an authentic plea to be left alone to study and a shunning of the materialistic. The sonnet form gives full rein to Juana's debating skills and Espaillat relinquishes not a beat in her version: "best of all truths I hold this truth to be:/cast all the vanities of life away,/and not your life away on vanity."

But surely true love, of some kind, beats in so many of these verses. "In Pain as from a Mortal Wound" begins with broken-heartedness. But it is Juana's trademark that she ends on rationality. Elsewhere, the speaker of these poems reveals a passion that tells us she was far from a bloodless "blue-stocking":

"If it is fated that your charms must be
magnets to the true steel of my heart's core,
why court me sweetly, flatter and implore,
and then laugh at my grief and run from me?"

("Halt, Dearest Shadow Always Poised to Flee")

5

Yet she ends on the primacy of her own ability to construct a "cell" of fantasy that cannot be destroyed. The notion of the life of the mind was unfailingly strong in the poet.

Her long poem "The Charge" sets her up as critic of the mores of her time and place. The speaker calls out the hypocrisy of men (and perhaps, more generally, society) in the double-standards set for women: "The girl with all the right moves/is the one trawling the corner,/but in the morning he'll scorn her: she's not the type he approves."

And yet, despite the secular sonnets written to and about so many, despite the busyness of her nun's cell, Sor Juana's most personal poem is ultimately geared to God. Like Sappho, Juana is often dubbed the "tenth muse." Her relentless antenna for knowledge, her uncanny capacity and thirst to see connections between things, make her a poet. And poets are always (consciously or not) would-be imitators of God who sees, as no one else can, the interconnected fabric of all things. Juana herself was very much aware of learning as a route to approaching the mysteries of the Divine—indeed, this is how she justified herself in her "Response" to the bishop's criticism. But could her justification have been just a handy way of defending her work? It seems not, for the "Response" shows us that she knew very well that learning was a way of drawing closer to God. Knowledge of astronomy, she wrote, and music, and all the arts and sciences, aid us in our reading of Scripture. How else can we understand David's harp or the measurements of Jerusalem?

Juana's "First Dream" is not only her most personal poem, it is also her most modern. In this radical piece Juana, like her namesake John of the Cross, uses night as an escape through which her soul is let loose to seek knowledge. Unlike Saint John, who unites mystically with God, Juana seeks to grasp everything about the universe. The life of the poem lies in the soul's act of seeking truth—but its comprehension of all things is necessarily limited by human constraints and hubris. The poem begins with an extraordinary depiction of night falling and the emergence of the "triple-faced" goddess—the moon (translated here). Espaillat also translates a telling passage from later in this piece, which is a kind of dare from Juana to herself to pursue learning even at the risk of a very sorry ending.

How much Juana's own ending was sorry is hard to know. Writing and studying had been as necessary to her as air and water. They were the core of her vocation. Was her self-recrimination written in blood sincere? Was her silence chosen? Or was it necessary self-censorship in an age of misogyny and Inquisition? She died nursing a plague victim—a fate more usually associated with the holy than the artistic.

We cannot know how resignedly she turned to those great silences, service to others, and death. We can only read with awe the writings of this woman who protested that women should have access to education, and defended the sacred nature of learning; who was able to speak so deftly of matters of the heart. We can only be glad that the flame of the "Phoenix of the Americas" was able to burn

7

for the time that it did, and that its brightness allows us to see it today in these dazzling translations.

—SALLY READ

A Word from the Translator . . . and a Mexican Nun:

Writing has brought me a vast fortune. No, not in dollars, pesos, francs, or rubles, but in a currency much older and infinitely more stable than any other: the unfailing friendship, trust, encouragement, and good will of people who have taught me to live and work in two languages, and even dabble in others.

The names that come to my memory at once span many decades and represent the mix of the Americas: Alfred Dorn and Dana Gioia demonstrating tirelessly that literature is the first universal language of the human race; Silvio Torres-Saillant, Mike Juster, and Nancy Kang creating bridges out of our differences, rather than weapons; my "Miss Jones" and Debbie Szabo in their Creative Writing classes proving to the young that education is the soul's daily bread; Kevin Wery, Juan Matos, and Vicki Hendrickson scheming to spread learning far beyond the classroom and way past youth; Leslie Monsour, John Tavano, David Yang, Rikka Pietalainen, and Ryan Turner enriching the arts by linking them and making them an essential part of every life . . . and many others.

This book—my English translations of the poems of Sor Juana Inés de la Cruz, the Mexican nun who struggled for education, not for herself alone but for untaught women everywhere—is dedicated to Alfred Nicol, who has done every one of the things noted above, as poet, critic, teacher, translator, lyricist, and member of a musical group, and, to me, an invaluable guide, support, and pal.

Thank you, Alfred, from Sor Juana and me!

Mi corazón deshecho entre tus manos

versos de Sor Juana Inés de la Cruz

The Liquid Pour in which my Heart has Run

Poems by Sor Juana Inés de la Cruz

¿En perseguirme, mundo, qué interesas?

Quéjase de la suerte: insinua su aversión a los vicios, y justifica su divertimiento a las Musas.

¿En perseguirme, mundo, qué interesas?
¿En qué te ofendo, cuando sólo intento
poner bellezas en mi entendimiento
y no mi entendimiento en las bellezas?

Yo no estimo tesoros no riquezas,
y así, siempre me causa más contento,
poner riquezas en mi pensamiento
que no mi pensamiento en las riquezas.

Yo no estimo hermosura que vencida
es despojo civil de las edades
ni riqueza me agrada fementida,

teniendo por mejor en mis verdades
consumir vanidades de la vida
que consumir la vida en vanidades.

When You Pursue Me, World

She complains of her fate, claims aversion to
luxuries, and declares her pleasure in the Muses.

When you pursue me, world, why do you do it?
How do I harm you, when my sole intent
is to make learning my prize ornament,
not learn to prize ornament and pursue it?

I have no treasure, and I do not rue it,
since all my life I have been most content
rendering mind—by learning—opulent,
not minding opulence, rendering tribute to it.

I have no taste for beauties that decay
and are the spoil of ages as they flee,
nor do those riches please me that betray;

best of all truths I hold this truth to be:
cast all the vanities of life away,
and not your life away on vanity.

A la esperanza

Verde embeleso . . .

Verde embeleso de la vida humana,
    loca esperanza, frenesí dorado,
sueño de los despiertos intrincado,
    como de sueños, de tesoros vana;

alma del mundo, senectud lozana,
    decrépito verdor imaginado;
el hoy de los dichosos esperado
y de los desdichados el mañana:

    sigan tu sombra en busca de tu día
los que, con verdes vidrios por anteojos,
    todo lo ven pintado a su deseo;

que yo, más cuerda en la fortuna mía,
tengo en entrambas manos ambos ojos
    y solamente lo que toco veo.

To Hope

She doubts the wisdom of unrealistic hope.

Green spell that so beguiles humanity,
unreasoning hope, gilded delirium,
dream that the sleepless dream, unrescued from
the fantasy of fortunes not to be;

soul of the world, old age dressed handsomely,
imaginary blossoming of some
bare branch, the lucky man's today—"to come
tomorrow," says the luckless man, "for me":

Let them who will follow and live for you,
those who, green-spectacled, pursue in vain
chimaeras they create and trust too much.

Saner about my fate, I keep my two
eyes in my two hands, and find it plain
there's nothing I can see but what I touch.

Con el dolor de la mortal herida

Con el dolor . . .

Con el dolor de la mortal herida,
de un agravio de amor me lamentaba,
y por ver si la muerte se llegaba
procuraba que fuese más crecida.
Toda en su mal el alma divertida,
pena por pena su dolor sumaba,
y en cada circunstancia ponderaba
que sobraban mil muertes a una vida.
Y cuando, al golpe de uno y otro tiro
rendido el corazón, daba penoso
señas de dar el último suspiro.
no sé por que destino prodigioso
volví a mi acuerdo y dije: ¿que me admiro?
¿Quién en amor ha sido más dichoso?

In Pain as from a Mortal Wound

She learns—and accepts—the inevitable pain
that accompanies love.

In pain as from a mortal wound, I cried,
lamenting how Love did me injury,
and wished approaching death would set me free
if agony were only amplified.
My soul, with pain alone preoccupied,
tallied its sum of griefs incessantly,
concluding that a single life must be
a thousand deaths endured, and more beside.
And now, after another blow, my heart,
going down in defeat, uttered a sigh,
contemplating the end. But with a start
I turned toward reason—though I don't know why;
recalled—and told myself—this wiser part:
Who has been luckier in love than I?

Al que ingrato

*Prosigue el mismo asunto, y determina que
prevalezca la razón contra el gusto.*

Al que ingrato me deja, busco amante;
al que amante me sigue, dejo ingrata;
constante adoro a quien mi amor maltrata;
maltrato a quien mi amor busca constante.
Al que trato de amor, hallo diamante.
y soy diamante al que de amor me trata;
triunfante quiero ver al que me mata,
y mato a quien me quiere ver triunfante.
Si a éste pago, padece mi deseo;
sí ruego a aquél, mi pundonor enojo:
de entrambos modos infeliz me veo.
Pero yo por mejor partido escojo,
de quien no quiero, ser violento empleo,
que de quien no me quiere, vil despojo.

Ingrates Who Flee Me

She concludes that reason ought to outweigh desire.

Ingrates who flee me feed my love more fuel,
but lovers seek me, and—ingrate!—I flee;
who scorns my love I adore instantly;
toward who adores me, constantly I'm cruel.
The object of my love I find a jewel,
and he who loves me finds a jewel in me;
to him who kills me I wish victory,
but kill the one who hands me the right tool.
If I reward the one, desire must die;
crawl to the other, and my honor sues.
Trapped between both, how miserable am I!
But there's a best alternative I choose:
for him I love not, violence to try:
from him who loves me not, trash to refuse.

El ausente, el celoso, se provoca

Sólo con aguda ingeniosidad esfuerza el dictamen
de que sea la ausencia mayor mal que los celos.

El ausente, el celoso, se provoca,
aquél con sentimiento, éste con ira;
presume éste la ofensa que no mira,
y siente aquél la realidad que toca.
 Ésta templa, tal vez, su furia loca
cuando el discurso en su favor delira,
y sin intermisión aquél suspira,
pues nada a su dolor la fuerza apoca.
 Éste aflige dudoso su paciencia,
u aquél padece ciertos sus desvelos;
éste al dolor opone resistencia,
 aquél, sin ella, sufre desconsuelos;
y si es pena de daño, al fin, la ausencia,
luego es mayor tormento que los celos.

The Absent and the Jealous

*She concludes that absence causes greater sorrow
than jealousy.*

The absent and the jealous suffer much:
the first from feeling, and the last from ire;
one over unseen crimes believed entire,
the other over felt things he can touch.
This one tempers his ire, when such-and-such
seems to be echoing his own desire;
that one sighs constantly when hope—that liar—
offers but grants no faith to serve as crutch.
This one has patience which he learns to doubt,
that one in pain suffers his nights awake.
This one visits what every day's about,
that one has no resistance to the ache;
and if hope, lost, from God keeps us without,
absence indeed must be the worst mistake.

Fabio, en el ser de todos adoradas

Enseña cómo un solo empleo en amar es razón y conveniencia

Fabio, en el ser de todos adoradas
son todas las beldades ambiciosas,
porque tienen las aras por ociosas
si no las ven de víctimas colmadas.

    Y así, si de uno solo son amadas,
viven de la fortuna querellosas;
porque piensan que más que ser hermosas
constituye deidad el ser rogadas.

    Mas yo soy en aquesto tan medida,
que en viendo a muchos mi atención zozobra
sólo quiero ser correspondida.

    de aquel que de mi amor réditos cobra;
porque es la sal del gusto al ser querido:
que daña lo que falta, y lo que sobra.

Fabio, in Truth, it is the Wish of All

She believes that love imposes one sole and reasonable duty.

Fabio, in truth, it is the wish of all
beauties to be adored, and thus renowned,
as those not seen by many victims crowned
are seen as idlers with no prize in thrall.
It's true, if but one man is seen to fall,
love-struck, before a woman, she is found
complaining of her fate, and failure-bound,
because she thinks just one a sum too small.
But, measuring, I have such care observed
that seeing many, my perception wanes:
I want only mutuality, deserved
by one who treasures love for its true gains.
Being loved, like too much salt, spoils what is served,
and, if it's not enough, spoils what remains.

Que no me quiera Fabio

Resuelve la cuestión de cuál sea pesar más molesto
en encontradas correspondencias, amar o aborrecer

Que no me quiera Fabio, al verse amado,
es dolor sin igual en mi sentido;
mas, que me quiera Silvio aborrecido,
es menor mal, mas no menor enfado.

¿Qué sufrimiento no estará cansado
si siempre le resuenan al oído,
tras la vana arrogancia de un querido,
el cansado gemir de un desdeñado?

Si de Silvio me cansa el rendimiento,
a Fabio canso con estar rendida;
si de éste busco el agradecimiento,

a mi me busca el otro agradecida:
por active y pasiva es mi tormento,
pues padezco en querer y en ser querida.

Fabio, Who Knows I Love Him

She decides which is more difficult in a personal
relationship: to adore or detest the other.

Fabio, who knows I love him, loves me not:
nothing else I can feel causes such pain.
Silvio, who plagues me with his love in vain,
gives me less grief, but keeps my temper hot.
What suffering won't wear you out that's got
you grieving over arrogant disdain
from one you love, or driving you insane
with moans from one you care for not a jot?
If Silvio makes me sick with his pursuing,
I know I sicken Fabio with pursuit;
I expect thanks from Fabio for my wooing;
Silvio wants thanks for what's not worth a hoot.
That's "passive/active" punishment for doing
both: giving and getting love: the double route!

Feliciano me adora, y le aborrezco

Continua el asunto, y aun le expresa con más viva elegancia.

Feliciano me adora y le aborrezco;
Lisardo me aborrece y yo le adoro;
por quien no me apetece ingrato, lloro,
y al que me llora tierno, no apetezco:
   A quien más me desdora, el alma ofrezco;
a quien me ofrece víctimas, desdoro;
desprecio al que enriquece mi decoro
y al que le hace desprecios enriquezco;
si con mi ofensa al uno reconvengo,
me reconviene el otro a mí ofendido
y al padecer de todos modos vengo;
pues ambos atormentan mi sentido:
aquéste con pedir lo que no tengo
y aquél con no tener lo que le pido.

Feliciano, Who Adores Me, I Despise

The theme continues, and is expressed with even more lively elegance.

Feliciano, who adores me, I despise;
Lisardo, who abhors me, I adore.
For those I cannot tempt, what tears I pour!
But those who weep for me . . . don't appetize.
For who makes me look bad in others' eyes,
my soul; nothing for him who spreads before
me, say, victims; grovelers never score.
But ruin my reputation? Here's your prize.
If I offend one and have lots to rue,
the other's trouble too, since either one
creates tangles the mind has to undo,
and both torment me with no place to run,
one begging for what I've no access to,
and one denying me his store of none.

Redondillas

*Arguye de inconsecuente el gusto y la censura
de los hombres, que en las mujeres acusan lo
que causan*

Hombres necios que acusáis
a la mujer sin razón,
sin ver que sois la ocasión,
de lo mismo que culpáis;

si con ansia sin igual
solicitáis su desden,
¿por qué queréis que obren bien,
si las incitáis al mal?

Combatís su resistencia,
y luego, con gravedad,
decis que fue liviandad
lo que hizo la diligencia.

Stanzas: The Charge

She charges men with senseless injustice, because
they blame women for the errors and flaws that
men themselves cause.

How brainless you men can be,
blaming women just because
you can't see it's your own paws
wreak the havoc you can see!

With wild insistence you hound them
until they drink more and wear less:
why be shocked when they grow careless,
not modest, the way you found them?

You fight them when they resist you,
and later, with a straight face,
claim they proved they're a disgrace
when they hugged you tight and kissed you.

Parecer quiere el denuedo
de vuestro parecer loco,
al niño que pone el coco
y luego le tiene miedo.

Queréis, con presunción necia,
hallar a la que buscáis,
para pretendida, Tais,
y en la posesión, Lucrecia.

¿Que humor puede ser más raro
que el falto de consejo,
él mismo empaña el espejo,
y siente que no esté claro?

Con el favor y desdén
tenéis condición igual,
quejándoos, si os tratan mal,
burlándoos, si os quieren bien.

You're like the toddler whose prize
is the pumpkin carved and lit,
and then has a crying fit,
frightened by its scary eyes.

The girl with all the right moves
is the one trawling the corner,
but in the morning he'll scorn her:
she's not the type he approves.

Can anything be more weird
than slopping mirrors with slime,
complaining at the same time
that the mirrors are all smeared?

Hard to tell which you prefer:
rejected, you moan and whine;
but if she falls for your line,
it's a joke, and it's on her.

Opinión ninguna gana.
Pues la que más se recata,
si no os admite, es ingrata,
y si os admite, es liviana.

Siempre tan necios andáis
que, con desigual nivel,
a una culpáis por cruel,
y a otra por fácil culpáis.

¿Pues cómo ha de estar templada
la que vuestro amor pretende,
si la que es ingrata, ofende,
y la que es fácil, enfada?

Mas entre el enfado y pena
que vuestro gusto refiere,
bien haya la que no os quiere,
y quejaos en hora buena.

The loser's always her part:
if she's careful of her honor
she's heartless: a curse upon her.
If she'll have you, she's a tart.

You sneak around, mean and sleazy,
all unjustly laying blame:
one gets "teaser" for a name,
and the other's known as "easy."

How can a woman stay true
when the "thankless" will offend,
and who takes you for a friend
will regret playing with you?

Well, between anger and sorrow—
whichever may be your lot—
good luck to who loves you not:
enjoy complaining tomorrow.

Dan vuestras amantes penas
a sus libertades alas,
y después de hacerlas malas,
las queréis hallar muy buenas.

¿Cuál mayor culpa ha tenido
en una pasión errada,
la que cae de rogada,
o el que ruega de caido?

¿O cuál es más de culpar,
aunque cualquiera mal haga
la que peca por la paga,
o el que paga por pecar?

Your lovers, made to feel free
of constraints, may fly away.
But once you've taught them to stray,
you want what they used to be!

When love goes wrong, after all,
tell me who is more to blame:
she who fell deep into shame,
or he who coaxed her to fall?

Or which has guiltier been—
none is guiltless all his days—
she who sins because he pays,
or he who pays her to sin?

¿Pues para qué os espantáis
de la culpa que tenéis?
Queredlas cual las hacéis,
o hacedlas cual las buscais.

Dejad de solicitar,
y después, con más razón,
acusaréis la afición
de la que os fuere a rogar.

Bien con muchas armas fundo
que lidia vuestra arrogancia,
pues en promesa e instancia,
juntáis diablo, carne y mundo.

Why, then, discover with fright
the debt that you surely owe?
Love them, you who made them so,
or make them as you think right.

Give up insisting she do
what's wrong. Rather, justly then
blame her with more reason when
she tries cuddling up to you.

With powerful proofs I level
this charge: you are armed for war
with stubborn pride, pleas, and more:
the world, the flesh, and the devil.

Detente, sombra de mi bien esquivo

Que contiene una fantasia contenta con amor decente.

Detente, sombra de mi bien esquivo,
imagen del hechizo que más quiero,
bella ilusión por quien alegre muero,
dulce ficción por quien penosa vivo.
Si al imán de tus gracias, atractivo,
sirve mi pecho de obediente acero,
¿para qué me enamoras lisonjero
si has de burlarme luego fugitivo?
Mas blasonar no puedes, satisfecho,
de que triunfa de mí tu tiranía:
que aunque dejas burlado el lazo estrecho
que tu forma fantástica ceñía,
poco importa burlar brazos y pecho
si te labra prisión mi fantasía.

Halt, Dearest Shadow Always Poised to Flee

She counts on the power of fantasy in the service of love.

Halt, dearest shadow always poised to flee,
spellbinding vision that I most adore,
fair dream I willingly would perish for,
sweet lie for which I live in misery.
If it is fated that your charms must be
magnets to the true steel of my heart's core,
why court me sweetly, flatter and implore,
and then laugh at my grief and run from me?
But never mind: you shall not boast you have
triumphed, or that your power is complete:
you may escape the strict confinement of
bonds you evade and vanquish with deceit—
but though my arms and breast may lose your love,
fantasy builds a cell you cannot cheat.

Tan grande, ¡ay hado!

Muestre sentir que la baldonen por los aplausos de su habilidad.

¿Tan grande, ¡ay hado!, mi delito ha sido
que por castigo de él, o por tormento,
no basta el que adelanta el pensamiento,
sino el que le previenes al oído?
Tan severo en mi contra has procedido
que me persuado de tu duro intento,
a que sólo me diste entendimiento
porque fuese mi daño más crecido.
Dísteme aplausos para más baldones,
subirme hiciste para penas tales;
y aun pienso que me dieron tus traiciones
penas a mi desdicha desiguales
porque, viéndome rica de tus dones,
nadie tuviese lástima a mis males.

So Great, O Fortune!

How it wounds her to be insulted for the praise earned by her abilities.

So great, O fortune! has my trespass been
that I must suffer, not the punishment
of thought alone, but of the malice sent
into my ear, to wound me with its din?
So harshly am I treated, I begin
to understand with what unkind intent
you deigned to render me intelligent
only to charge me dearly for that sin.
Applause you gave, that I might be maligned:
exalted me, toward greater pain tomorrow;
dealt with me so perfidiously I find
your ill will doubles what ill luck I borrow,
so that, rich in those gifts you gave my mind,
I earn nobody's pity for my sorrow.

Esta tarde, mi bien

En que satisface un recelo con la retorica del llanto.

Esta tarde, mi bien, cuando te hablaba,
como en tu rostro y tus acciones vía
que con palabras no te persuadía,
que el corazón me vieses deseaba;

y Amor, que mis intentos ayudaba,
venció lo que imposible parecía:
pues entre el llanto, que el dolor vertía,
el corazón deshecho destilaba.

Baste ya de rigores, mi bien, baste:
no te atormenten más celos tiranos,
ni el vil recelo tu quietud contraste

con sombras necias, con indicios vanos,
pues ya en liquido humor viste y tocaste
mi corazón deshecho entre tus manos.

Today, My Treasure

She attempts to heal a jealous lover with the rhetoric of tears.

Today, my treasure, when I said my part,
since in your face and gestures I perceived
that all my words, though true, were not believed,
I longed to let you see my naked heart;

and Love, who lent assistance to my art,
what seemed at first impossible achieved:
for as the tears flowed more the more I grieved,
my heart dissolved away and oozed apart.

No more of all this anger, love, no more:
let every doubt that troubles you be banned—
those phantom fears that wound you to the core,

those lying signs that your suspicions fanned—
since you have seen and felt the liquid pour
in which my heart has run into your hand.

Amor empieza por desasosiego

Que consuela a un celoso, epilogando la serie de los amores.

Amor empieza por desasosiego,
solicitud, ardores y desvelos;
crece con riesgos, lances y recelos;
susténtase de llantos y de ruego.
Doctrínanle tibiezas y despego,
conserva el ser entre engañosos velos,
hasta que con agravios o con celos
apaga con sus lágrimas su fuego.
Su principio, su medio y fin es éste:
¿pues por qué, Alcino, sientes el desvío
de Celia, que otro tiempo bien te quiso?
¿Qué razón hay de que dolor te cueste?
Pues no te engaño amor, Alcino mío,
sino que llegó el término preciso.

Love Has Its Early Stirrings in Unease

She consoles a jealous lover by summarizing the normal course of love.

Love has its early stirrings in unease,
in care, in passion's fire and wakefulness;
it grows through quarrels, trials and doubt's distress,
and feeds on sorrow, pleading on its knees.
Disdain then tutors it, and hard-to-please
indifference in deceit's seductive dress,
till jealousy, or grief beyond excess,
draws tears to quench the flames none can appease.
Since such is Love's beginning, mid and close,
why mourn, Alcino, that your Celia's left
you now, who loved you once? Alcino, friend,
what cause have you to suffer, since Love goes,
not like a cheat after committing theft,
but having reached its one and proper end?

Dices que yo te olvido, Celio, y mientes.

No quiere pasar por olvido lo descuidado.

Dices que yo te olvido, Celio, y mientes,
en decir que me acuerdo de olvidarte,
pues no hay en mi memoria alguna parte
en que, aun como olvidado, te presentes.
Mis pensamientos son tan diferentes
y en todo tan ajenos de tratarte,
que ni saben ni pueden agraviarte,
ni si te olvidan saben si lo sientes.
Si tú fueras capaz de ser querido,
fueras capaz de olvido; y ya era gloria
al menos la potencia de haber sido.
Mas tan lejos estás de esa victoria,
que aqueste no acordarme no es olvido
sino una negación de la memoria.

You Say that I Forget You, But You Lie

Clori to Celio, who won't accept being "forgotten."

You say that I forget you, but you lie:
it would require thinking to forget you,
and nowhere in my thinking have I let you—
even as one forgotten—saunter by.
My thoughts are far—so far—from you, that I,
focused elsewhere, as if I'd never met you,
have no idea what thoughts of mine upset you,
or if your absence from them makes you sigh.
If anyone could love you, one could, yes,
forget you: what a triumph that would be,
affirming your existence; none the less,
you are so far from such a victory
that you're eclipsed, not through forgetfulness,
but sheer rejection by my memory.

Dices, que no te acuerdas, Clori, y mientes

Sin perder los mismos consonantes, contradice con la
verdad, aun mas ingeniosa, su hiperbole.

Dices, que no te acuerdas, Clori, y mientes
en decir, que te olvidas de olvidarte;
pues das ya en tu memoria alguna parte,
en que, por olvidado, me presentes.
Si son tus pensamientos diferentes
de los de Albiro, dejarás tratarte;
pues tu misma pretendes agraviarte,
con querer persuadir, lo que no sientes.
Niégasme ser capaz de ser querido,
y tú misma concedes esta gloria,
con que en tu contra tu argumento ha sido.
Pues si para alcanzar tanta victoria,
te acuerdas de olvidarte del olvido,
ya no das negación a tu memoria.

You Claim to Have Forgotten Me, But Lie

Celio replies, using the same rhymes in refutation.

You claim to have forgotten me, but lie
when you say, "I've forgotten to forget you,"
since clearly, thinking so, your mind won't let you
forget forgotten me, and keeps me by.
If your thoughts differ from Albiro's, I
suspect you'll come around, for since I met you
it's you who think the thoughts that most upset you,
saying things you don't mean that make you sigh.
You say that I'm not lovable, but yes,
it's you yourself who prove I well may be,
so all your arguments profit you less
than they do me; since to gain victory
you keep forgetting your forgetfulness,
I'm not rejected by your memory.

Miró Celia una rosa que en el prado

Escoge antes el morir que exponerse a los ultrajes de la vejez.

Miró Celia una rosa que en el prado
ostentaba feliz la pompa vana,
y con afeites de carmín y grana
bañaba alegre el rostro delicado;
    y dijo: Goza sin temor del hado
el curso breve de tu edad lozana,
pues no podrá la muerte de mañana
quitarte lo que hubieres hoy gozado.
    Y aunque llega la muerte presurosa
y tu fragrante vida se te aleja,
no sientes el morir tan bella y moza:
    mira que la experiencia te aconsejo
que es fortuna morirte siendo hermosa
y no ver el ultraje de ser vieja.

Celia Had Found a Proud Rose

Celia chooses early death rather than risking the ravages wrought by old age.

Celia had found a proud rose in the field,
vaunting with joy and vanity the sheen—
crimson and scarlet—that the maid had seen.
And later, with the brush that beauties wield,
applied like brushes delicately sealed
to silken skin, and said, "Enjoy, serene,
fearless of fate, which in due time may mean
to end your present joy. You need not yield,
even if death itself will one day rush
to take the fragrant, pleasant life you know.
"Do not regret that early death may crush
your youth: experience says it's better so,
lucky to die while beautiful and lush,
before old age deals its horrendous blow."

Si los riesgos del mar considerara

Encarece de animosidad la elección de estado durable hasta la muerte.

Si los riesgos del mar considerara,
ninguno se embarcara, si antes viera
bien su peligro, nadie se atreviera,
ni al bravo toro asado provocara;
    si del fogoso bruto ponderara
la furia desbocada en la carrera
el jinete prudente, nunca hubiera,
quien con discreta mano le enfrenara.
    Pero si hubiera alguno tan osado
que, no obstante el peligro, al mismo Apolo
quisiere gobernar con atrevida
    mano el rápido carro en luz bañado,
todo lo hiciera; y no tomara sólo
estado que ha de ser toda la vida.

If One Explored the Risks at Sea

Avoiding risk in favor of endless life makes for timidity; to accept driving Apollo's chariot risks all but living forever.

If one explored the risks at sea, none ever
would choose to go by water, once aware
of all the dangers, nor would any dare,
if prudent, to incite the bull, that clever,
brave beast who seems by nature never
less than a fiery runner none would care
to halt in mid-career and master there.
But if one brave enough were to endeavor
driving Apollo's speedy light-bathed car
with hands daring enough to navigate,
then he alone would face what risks there are;
he would do anything, not hesitate,
and from his deeds alone the one he'd bar
would be the lifelong one of endless date.

Primero sueño (versos 1-18)

Piramidal, funesta de la tierra
nacida sombra, al cielo encaminaba
de vanos obeliscos punta altiva,
escalar pretendiendo las estrellas;
si bien sus luces bellas
      exemptas siempre, siempre rutilantes,
      la tenebrosa guerra
que con negros vapores le intimaba
la vaporosa sombra fugitiva
      burlaban tan distantes,
      que su atezado ceño
al superior convexo aún no llegaba
      del orbe de la diosa
que tres veces hermosa
      con tres hermosos rostros ser ostenta;
      quedando sólo o dueño
del aire que empañaba
      con el aliento denso que exhalaba.

First Dream (Lines 1-18)

Pyramidal, born of the earth, ill-fated,
a shadow rose toward the sky, attempting flight
on tips of obelisks, whose wish, unsated,
was to invade the realm of every star;
and there the stars, in their own lovely light,
      forever free, forever gleaming,
        saw grim warfare coming now
in cloudy blackness as of vapors steaming;
but soon they mocked the faint, fugitive shade,
      because its burnished brow,
      advancing, seemed so far
from the outermost sphere of the goddess who
      thrice beautiful had been made,
and with her three faces wore her beauty, too.
      The invader, left all alone,
      had nothing more to own
than temporary breaths of borrowed air
      he rendered dense while there.

Primero sueño (versos 781-826)

Otras—más esforzado—,
demasiada acusaba cobardia
el lauro antes ceder, que en la lid dura
haber siquiera entrado;
y al ejamplar osado
del claro joven la atención volvía
—auriga altivo del ardiente carro—,
y el, si infeliz, bizarro
alto impulso, el espíritu encendía:
donde el ánimo halla
—más que el temor ejemplos de escarmiento—
abiertas sendas al atrevimiento,
que una ya vez trilladas, no hay castigo
que intento baste a remover segundo
(segunda ambición, digo).

First Dream (Lines 781-826)

At other times—more daring—
the mind condemned it as excessive fear
to forfeit victory beforehand by
avoiding all warfaring;
then mind bent to comparing
that course with the man's who dared to steer
the burning chariot; his deed invited
misfortune, but ignited
the spirit's flame to match the charioteer
until at last it led to,
not cause for fear, but lessons to be learned
and pathways to the risks for which it yearned:
roads which, once taken, fear of punishment
would never keep untraveled—so I say—
by repetitive intent.

Ni el panteón profundo
—cerúlea tumba a su infeliz ceniza—,
ni el vengativo rayo fulminante
mueve, por más que avisa,
al ánimo arrogante
que, el vivir despreciando, determina
su nombre eternizar en su ruina.
Tipo es, antes, modelo:
ejemplar pernicioso
que alas engendra a repetido vuelo,
del ánimo ambicioso
que—del mismo terror haciendo halago
que al valor lisonjea—
las glorias deletrea
entre los caracteres del estrago.

Not the deep where he must stay—
cerulean grave of his unhappy ashes—
nor that destroying ray of vengeful fire
in any way abashes
the arrogant desire
of those who think it worthless to draw breath
unless they glorify their names in death.
Rather may example spur
the overly ambitious
the same high-flying peril to incur,
through flattery's pernicious
urging, which sends courage to seek glory
in those very risks that spell
ruin, and, read right, foretell
only disastrous endings to the story.

O el castigo jamás se publicara,
porque nunca el delito se intentara:
politico silencio antes rompiera
los autos del proceso
—circunspecto estadista—;
o en fingida ignorancia simulara
o con secreta pena castigara
el insolente exceso,
sin que a popular vista
el ejemplar nocivo propusiera:
que del mayor delito la malicia
peligra en la noticia
contagio dilatado trascendiendo;
porque singular culpa sólo siendo,
dejara más remota a lo ignorado
su ejecución, que no a lo escarmentado.

O, would that punishments were never touted!
the motive for such crime should then be flouted:
Judicious silence should—statesman most wise—
wholly put an end at once
to every rash endeavor,
or manage to feign ignorance about it,
or else, by punishing in secret, rout it
in those charged with such affronts,
without displaying, ever,
noxious examples before others' eyes.
For from insolent deeds the greatest trouble
is how, through fame, they double,
spreading contagion where the deed is known;
when guilt is single, distant and alone,
less likelihood exists of imitation
than when harsh punishments draw admiration.

Soneto 185

¡Oh cuán frágil se muestra el ser humano
en los últimos términos fatales,
donde sirven aromas Orientales
de culto inútil, de resguardo vano!

Sólo a ti respetó el poder tirano,
¡oh gran Felipe!, pues con las señales
que ha mostrado que todos son mortales,
te ha acreditado a ti de Soberano.

Conoces ser de tierra fabricado
este cuerpo, y que está con mortal guerra
el bien del alma en él aprisionado;

y así, subiendo al bien que el Cielo encierra,
que en la tierra no cabes has probado,
pues aun tu cuerpo dejas porque es tierra.

Sonnet 185

On the Death of His Majesty King Philip IV

Oh, how frail mortal man is found to be
when he approaches this, his final day,
treated in vain with unguents from Cathay—
obeying false beliefs—all uselessly!

Only you have escaped death's tyranny,
great Philip! since despite its clear display
of the shared fate we may not disobey,
you have been crowned King by mortality.

You know that you are earth, since nothing more
of this, your body, which has been, since birth,
with your therein-imprisoned soul at war;

therefore, rising to Heaven's boundless worth,
you prove too great for Earth, since, as you soar,
you leave your body here, because it's earth.

Rosa divina

En que da moral censura a una rosa, y en ella a
sus semejantes.

Rosa divina que en gentil cultura
eres, con tu fragante sutileza,
magisterio purpúreo en la belleza,
enseñanza nevada a la hermosura.

Amago de la humana arquitectura,
ejemplo de la vana gentileza,
en cuyo ser unió naturaleza
la cuna alegre y triste sepultura.

¡Cuán altiva en tu pompa, presumida,
soberbia, el riesgo de morir desdeñas,
y luego desmayada y encogida

de tu caduco ser das mustias señas,
con que con docta muerte y necia vida,
viviendo engañas y muriendo enseñas!

Rose, Like a Goddess

In which a rose, like all her kind, is accused of dis-
honesty until her death.

Rose, like a goddess, bred to be refined
are you, enveloped in your subtle scent,
royally purple gorgeous wonderment,
snowy lesson in loveliness, designed

to prophesy how beauty is inclined
to lose what human fortune merely lent,
from joyful cradle to grave monument:
the ends that nature, from the start, combined.

How proud you are, with confidence endowed
that disbelieves death's power to leave you plucked
of arrogance and pomp, no longer proud.

Past your fool's life, wise death will leave you sucked
of all, a silent signal to the crowd:
I lied in life, but dying I instruct.

Este que ves, engaño colorido

Procura desmentir los elogios que a un retrato de la poetisa
inscribio la verdad, que llama pasion.

Este que ves, engaño colorido,
que, del arte ostentando los primores,
con falsos silogismos de colores
es cauteloso engaño del sentido;

éste, en quien la lisonja ha pretendido
excusar de los años los horrores,
y venciendo del tiempo los rigores
triunfar de la vejez y del olvido,

es un vano artificio del cuidado,
es una flor al viento delicada,
es un resguardo inútil para el hado:

es una necia diligencia errada,
es un afán caduco y, bien mirado,
es cadáver, es polvo, es sombra, es nada.

This That You See, This Brightly-Hued Pretense

In which Truth, personified, refutes the flatteries of art,
and inscribes her judgments on a portrait of the poet.

This that you see, this brightly-hued pretense,
here by the grace of art rendered appealing,
through specious feats of colorful deceiving
is cleverly deployed to cheat the sense;
this, in which flattery's munificence
has sought to mask the blows the years are dealing
so as to conquer time, thereby concealing
the horrors wrought by age and negligence,
is effort undertaken for no gain,
is a frail flower in the windy squall,
is a defense from fate mounted in vain,
is labor mad and wasted, doomed to fall,
is a fool's errand, and, regarded plain,
is corpse, is dust, is dark, is not at all.

Versions of the following poems first appeared in *Plough:*

"This That You See," January 14, 2023

"To Hope," January 14, 2023

"When You Pursue Me, World," December 6, 2022

Versions of the following first appeared in *New England Poetry Club* online journal under the title, *A Bout Rime Pair of Sonnets,* November 5, 2017:

"You Say That I Forget You, But You Lie"

"You Claim to Have Forgotten Me, But Lie"

"To Hope" was published by *Sewanee Theological Review,* Christmas 2012 issue.

About Sor Juana Inés de la Cruz

Nicknamed "The Tenth Muse," Sor Juana Inés de la Cruz (1648-1695) is considered the last great writer of the Hispanic Baroque period and the first great poet of the Americas. The illegitimate daughter of a Spanish officer and a wealthy criolla, Sor Juana was raised on her maternal grandfather's hacienda. Though education was forbidden for girls during this period, Sor Juana had access to her grandfather's extensive library. By three years of age, she taught herself to read and write Latin; by eight she wrote a poem on the Eucharist; and by adolescence, she mastered Greek logic.

At 16, she was sent to Mexico City to live with relatives. There she gained the patronage of the viceroy and vicereine of New Spain and her reputation as a poet, philosopher, dramatist, and scholar grew. With a desire "to have no fixed occupation which might curtail" her intellectual pursuits, as well as a "total disinclination to marriage," Sor Juana joined the Discalced Carmelites, later switching to the more lenient Hieronymite Order. Life in a cloistered convent afforded her time to focus on her own studies and writing, as well as teaching music and drama to girls in the convent school.

Sor Juana composed plays, philosophical treatises, and a remarkable range of other works, but it is her poetry, in particular, that is noted for its wit, inventiveness, and mastery of the poetic forms and themes of the Spanish Golden Age.

Despite the constrictions placed upon her, this singular woman has left us with a wide-ranging body of work that blazes with extraordinary brilliance and passion.

Sor Juana died in 1649 after contracting the plague while treating her fellow sisters.

Acerca del Traductior

Rhina P. Espaillat, dominicana de nacimiento y bilingue, es poeta, ensayista, cuentista y traductora, y fue por varios años maestra de inglés en las escuelas públicas secundarias de New York. Ha publicado doce libros, cinco libros de cordel, y un monógrafo sobre la traducción. Ha ganado varios premios nacionales e internacionales, y fue fundadora del grupo Fresh Meadows Poets en NYC y el grupo Powow River Poets en Newburyport. Sus obras más recientes son tres poemarios: *And After All*, *The Field*, y una collaboración con el poeta Alfred Nicol, *Brief Accident of Light: A Day in Newburyport*. Sus numerosas traducciones abarcan las obras de Sor Juana Inés de la Cruz, San Juan de la Cruz, Frederico García Lorca, Miguel Hernandez, Emily Dickinson, Walt Whitman, Robert Frost, Richard Wilbur, y muchos poetas contemporáneos de las Americas y la diáspora hispana, entre otros.

About the Translator

Dominican-born Rhina P. Espaillat is a bilingual poet, essayist, short story writer, translator, and former English teacher in New York City's public high schools. She has published twelve books, five chapbooks, and a monograph on translation. She has earned numerous national and international awards, and is a founding member of the Fresh Meadows Poets of NYC and the Powow River Poets of Newburyport, MA. Her most recent works are three poetry collections: *And After All, The Field,* and *Brief Accident of Light: A Day in Newburyport,* co-authored with Alfred Nicol. Her numerous translations include work by Sor Juana Inés de la Cruz, San Juan de la Cruz, Frederico García Lorca, Miguel Hernandez, Emily Dickinson, Walt Whitman, Robert Frost, Richard Wilbur, and many contemporary poets of the Americas and the Hispanic diaspora, among others.

ABOUT SALLY READ

Sally Read is the editor of "100 Great Catholic Poems" (Word on Fire, Nov 2023), and author of four collections of poetry, including the award-winning *Dawn of this Hunger*, her first publication of poetry since her conversion from atheism to Catholicism. Her poetry has been recorded for the UK's *Poetry Archive*, and her writing, in both poetry and prose, has appeared in numerous publications and anthologies, including *The Times Literary Supplement, The Independent on Sunday, The Manhattan Review,* and *The Picador Book of Love Poems.* Episodes of Sally's Radio Maria England show, "Poetry for the Season," are available on Spotify. Sally has also written two books of nonfiction: *Night's Bright Darkness* and *Annunciation: a Call to Faith in a Broken World.* Sally's work has been translated into five languages. A literary memoir, *The Mary Pages,* is forthcoming from Word on Fire in 2024.

Made in the USA
Middletown, DE
06 September 2023

38124224R00056